DISCOVERY

The Roman house was discovered, largely by cha
of the archaeological rescue excavations by the ....ological Rescue Unit
across the west side of Dover which began in 1970. With the pending construction
of the York Street bypass in a wide and deep cut and the subsequent large-scale
town centre redevelopment an intensive crash programme of excavation and
recording was launched in that year. It then seemed certain that any archaeological
structure or deposits over some eight acres would be totally destroyed. The work,
excavation, recording and publication has continued non-stop for 22 years and
most of the archaeological heritage discovered has since been saved.

One of many sites investigated by the team in 1970-1 was an area of overgrown
gardens of derelict houses (since demolished) on the north side of Market Street.
Designated as the site of a multi-storey car park, the gardens lay across the calculated
line of the west wall of the late Roman 'shore-fort'. A trial hole here in July 1970 found
not only slight traces of the fort wall, but also a painted wall of an unknown Roman
house. The discovery remained a closely guarded secret until July 1971 when a much
larger area, by now partly used as a temporary car park, was excavated. By August
Rooms 2, 3 and 4 had been fully excavated and by the end of September the site was
backfilled for protection. In 1972 another large scale excavation located the fort wall,
the bastion, the defensive ditch to the west and parts of Rooms 5 and 6. Room 1 was
excavated in 1975 and the passage to the north in 1976-7.

The Roman floors were located just 12ft. below the existing ground level and un-
disturbed soil at a depth of about 15ft. In all some 5,800 tons of soil and rubble were
removed by the archaeological team, enough to fill 580 10-yard lorries! Structures
and deposits earlier than the Painted House were found beneath it and more were
found at different levels in the soil above. The excavation also revealed that several
medieval cess-pits had been cut into the Roman building at about A.D.1300.

Of the various features of earlier or later date than the Painted House, the walls
of a smaller Roman building can be seen on the south and north sides.

This building, consisting of at least three rooms some with painted walls, was
probably an earlier house on the same site. Perhaps built in the middle part of the
2nd century A.D. it was largely demolished when the Painted House was built.
The soil beneath both these Roman houses was found to contain large quantities
of finely worked flint implements and flakes of the late Neolithic period. These
relate to an extensive settlement which covered the lower slopes of the Western
Heights at about 2000B.C.

ROOM 1

This room formed the east end of the Painted House and was flanked externally by a narrow metalled road. It was virtually identical in size, plan and detail to Room 2, but much less of it has survived. It contains a fine channelled hypocaust fed from a large arched flue on the south side and was originally plastered and painted. A door on the west side led into Room 2 and one on the north side into the passage.

At the time of the construction of the military fort across the Painted House, Room 1 remained in use, whereas Rooms 2 and 3 were buried under the rampart. The west doorway was closed by a chalk block wall and the vertical wall flues filled. The room seems to have remained in use for some considerable period as the wall plaster had decayed and was removed. A very small patch which remained indicates a red dado as in Room 3.

By about A.D.800 Room 1 was covered with about 4ft of soil and rubble. It was then that a sunken Anglo-Saxon hut was built partially across it thus creating a gap in the north wall. In the following centuries deep cess-pits cut through the centre and east wall of the room. What remained of the east wall of Room 1 was removed during the excavation to allow detailed study of its construction and to facilitate display.

Fig 1. The Painted House site just before the 1971 excavation.

Fig 2. The west side of Room 2 showing the painted panels.

ROOM 2

This is the most complete room surviving in the whole complex. It measures 18ft by 16ft and had doorways on the east and west sides leading to the adjacent rooms. Its walls still survive to a height of 4-6ft internally. This room was also heated by means of underfloor channels and hollow wall-ducts the source of heat again being a large arched flue in the south wall.

The internal walls were plastered and cleverly painted in bright colours. The lower section (the dado) was green, the central zone consisted of eighteen large rectangular panels with motifs of varying colours and forms and the upper area had been a frieze. Three medieval pits had later cut down into this room, one conveniently through the floor to reveal the central chamber of the heating system. Another pit removed the stone sill from the west doorway and another cut through the east wall.

Fig 3. The blocked doorway between Rooms 1 and 2.

On excavation the floor was found to be covered by a thin layer of fine mortar and fragmentary plaster, probably fallen from the ceiling above. Covering this on the west side was a deposit some 4ft thick of fallen plaster and rubble from the upper parts of the walls. The whole was covered by dumps of soil and rubble and a sealing layer of clay to create a rampart behind the later fort wall.

A COUNTRY WHICH DESTROYS ITS PAST
DESERVES TO HAVE NO FUTURE

ROOMS 3 and 4

There was no dividing wall between these two rooms and Room 4 was, in effect, a southern extension of Room 3. Both were substantially destroyed by the construction of the fort wall in about A.D.270. Room 3 was otherwise very much the same size as Rooms 1 and 2. It too had a channelled hypocaust, with similar wall flues, but its main furnace arch ran diagonally to the centre owing to the presence of Room 4.

Room 4 on the other hand was only about 10ft square and seems to have had no independent heating system. The heat from Room 3 would anyway have circulated into Room 4 as there was no wall between them, but just a wide opening flanked by narrow piers.

Of Room 4 only the east side and a small part of the south wall survive. These show a green dado and at least five more panels. Of Room 3 again, only the east wall and part of the north wall survive. The dado is red and parts of 5 panels remain.

ROOM 5

The greater part of Room 5 was destroyed by the army when digging their great defensive ditch on the outside of the later fort wall. Only parts of the south wall (projecting from under the bastion) and the east wall remain. This room too had a similar floor and heating system and traces of three damaged channels still survive. Its dado appears to have been red and its ceiling may have had similar plaster to Room 2.

ROOM 6

Only the south-east corner of this room survived the excavation of the fort ditch by the Roman soldiers. Its floor and green dado were similar to other rooms, but no trace of heating survived. Rather like Room 4 it appears to have been an extension to a larger room (here Room 5) to which it must have been connected by means of a doorway or larger opening.

PASSAGE

A narrow passage flanked the north side of Rooms 1-3 and much of this survives, though precisely what function it served is not altogether clear. A doorway led into it from Room 1 and it is just possible that another from Room 3 was removed when the later fort wall was built. Extensive traces of a series of rectilinear panels can be seen on one wall.

Fig 4. The panels in the north-west corner of Room 2.

Fig 5. The panels on the south wall of Room 2.

THE PAINTINGS

A detailed study of the painted plaster designs was published by the Kent Unit in 1989. This demonstrated that the overall design was dedicated to Bacchus the Roman God of Wine. It was framed within a monumental architectural scheme incorporating coloured bordered panels, clever perspective designs, human figures and other Bacchic motifs.

The general pattern follows a broad trend common elsewhere in Britain and in continental Europe. In this, the main walls were divided into three unequal parts. The lowest zone, perhaps about 2ft high, was the dado which was seldom highly decorated. At Dover the dado is either a deep red or green, each speckled with faint yellowish flecks of paint to imitate marble veneering. Immediately above the dado is an open field about 1ft high of mottled yellow-pink with an upper border of pinky red. Above this is the broad, main zone of decoration here about 3ft high. It consists of a whole series of rectangular panels, normally five on each wall. These panels have white backgrounds and coloured surround. The two corner panels have yellow surrounds, the inner two dark red surrounds and the centre panel one of an orange-pink. Each panel is separated from the next by a very finely painted column composed of a series of graded colours to imitate marble fluting and its shadows. These columns sit on rectangular bases, clearly outlined in red which themselves form part of a continuous stage, or podium, upon which the whole scene rests. As a deliberate attempt to give perspective, the four columns on each wall face away from the centre to varying degrees. The perspective effect is increased by subtle shadows behind each of the columns, the bases and the central motifs. The panels contain varying motifs, all originating it seems from the open field below the stage, again to help the three-dimensional effect. In Room 2 four yellow panels contained an orange 'torch' motif, the dark red panels a winding vine and the central panel perhaps some sort of vine growing from a bowl. The other walls seem to vary, with the substitution of at least a thyrsus, large fronds, a tympanon (hand drum) and in Room 4, a syrinx (Pipes of Pan), again all Bacchic related motifs.

The reconstructed fragments have also revealed parts of human figures. One standing male figure from Room 3, is perhaps Bacchus himself. A seated female figure, found in Room 2, could be Aridane, whilst three dancing female figures could be maenads, perhaps from the rooms above.

The tops of some of the panels were capped by elaborate entablature supported on the vertical columns. These created small projecting aediculae, forming major elements in the overall architectural scheme. The whole design on each wall was surmounted by a narrow frieze, mainly white but with a series of vertical slats in cream and also more motifs.

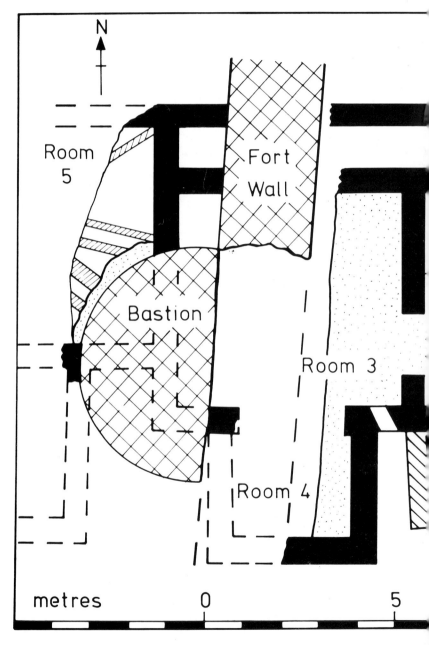

Fig 6. Plan showing the Painted House (A.D.200), e

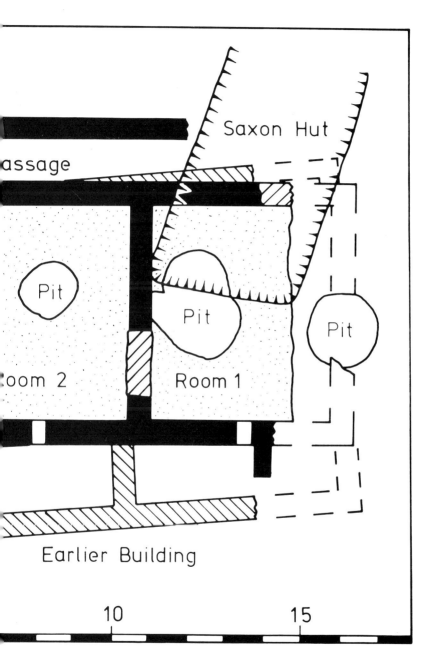

assage

Saxon Hut

Pit

Pit

Room 2

Room 1

Pit

Earlier Building

10   15

ilding (A.D.150) and later Saxon Hut (A.D.800).

HOW THE WALL PAINTINGS SURVIVED

Although many Roman buildings in Britain had walls painted in bright colours and designs, very little has survived, largely due to weathering and later damage. A few areas of fallen plaster have been located (notably at Lullingstone, York and Verulamium), but the limited survival of these has normally required very considerable reconstruction. At Dover, however, thanks to exceptional circumstances some 400 sq.feet of painted plaster survives 'in situ' which is more than in all the other structures in Britain. A large amount was also found in fragments on the Roman floors and carefully lifted.

The events which preserved the Dover plaster were highly unusual. The Roman house was requisitioned by the Roman army about A.D.270 whilst still in very good condition. The walls, rooms and all the plaster were then intact. The army engineers demolished part of the building and constructed a massive defensive fort wall through the middle of Rooms 3 and 4. What survived of Room 3 and all of Room 2 lay immediately behind the defensive wall in an area to become the rampart bank backing the fort wall. Rather than demolish these rooms to foundation level, the troops simply removed the upper parts of the walls and left the lower walls standing to a height of 6ft internally and 9ft externally. The rooms partially filled with rubble and broken plaster during this process and were then buried beneath a dump of soil and clay which formed the actual bank. This process completely sealed the painted walls in a matter of days or weeks and thus prevented deterioration by subsequent damage and weathering. Room 1, on the other hand, was not buried but remained in use for many years during which time the wall plaster disintegrated.

THE HEATING SYSTEM

The Painted House was designed and constructed with an elaborate system of underfloor and wall heating. In at least four of the rooms this was found substantially intact and followed an identical pattern. In each case the heat source, probably burning wood, originated close to the large furnace arch situated at or near the centre of one side of each room. From there a broad channel led to the middle of each room. From here the heat passed along seven more channels which led to the four corners and centres of the three other sides of the room. Each tapered channel (presumably to help induce a draught), led

Fig 7. The north-east corner of Room 3.

Fig 8. Detail of front and columns of Room 2.

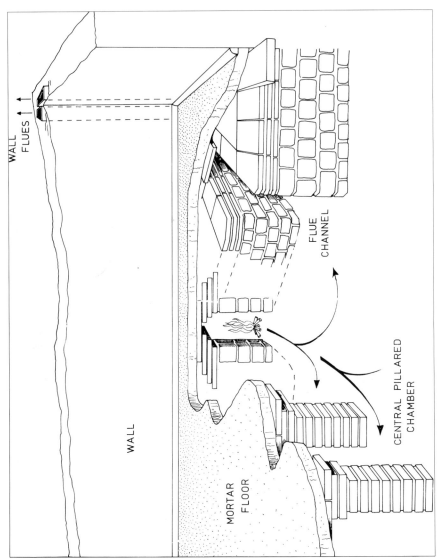

WALL
FLUES

WALL

MORTAR
FLOOR

FLUE
CHANNEL

CENTRAL PILLARED
CHAMBER

Fig 9. Sketch of heating system to show circulation of hot air under floors and inside walls.

to a vertical duct inside the walls, constructed by means of a series of hollow box-tiles placed on end. Again these survive in some detail in each room though exactly how the heat passed out of the top of the building is not clear. To allow the circulation of the hot air the floors had necessarily to be substantially hollow.

Fig 10. South wall of Painted House with furnace arches.

THE FORT WALL

By the third century A.D. the south-east shores of Britain were being invaded by Saxons from across the North Sea. The military response saw new Roman forts at Reculver, Brancaster and Caistor, Yarmouth and other forts were added decades later, notably at Richborough, Dover and Lympne in Kent. The system became known as the forts of the 'Saxon Shore'.

In A.D.270 the Roman army took over Dover (Dubris) and their engineers outlined an area of more than five acres enclosing or cutting through many earlier buildings. This was to be the site of the army fort, enclosed by a massive stone wall on all four sides. The west wall of this fort cut through Rooms 3 and 4 of the Painted House where it was 8ft wide and survives to a height of about 7ft. Although much robbed away over part of the site a length 16ft long still survives in the north area.

It was built of local materials. The external face usually consisted of neatly squared blocks of calcareous tufa and the internal face mostly of rough squared chalk blocks. The foundation consisted of irregular masses of stone, brick and mortar rubble mostly obtained from demolition of nearby buildings. The core of the wall was roughly constructed and also contained much re-used material.

THE BASTION

When the Roman army built its great fort across the area, its defensive wall included a small number of projecting towers, or bastions. These strengthened the walls and also provided high vantage points in terms of visibility and defence.

Under the original scheme the length of fort wall which crossed over the partially demolished Painted House was not fronted by bastions. However, within a few decades several bastions were added to the original fort at various points and one of these was placed across the remains of Rooms 5 and 6 of the Painted House. The lower 4ft-6ft of this great D-shaped bastion, about 20ft long and 12ft wide, still survives. It was added to the face of the pre-existing fort wall and when the wall was robbed away much later the bastion was somehow missed. Being built later, its construction was different from that of the fort wall. Its external face is mostly of flint and sandstone and there are two courses of tiles. The bastion was simply placed right on top of what survived of the Painted House and traces of the floor, wall and heating ducts of Room 5 can be seen projecting from beneath the plinth of the bastion.

Fig 11. Detail of the inside face of the fort wall during excavation.

THE SAXON HUT

It became clear as the excavation progressed that a large rectangular area, associated with layers of burnt debris, existed over the top of Room 1. Detailed investigation showed that in about A.D.800 some five centuries after the Painted House had become buried by the fort rampart and dumps of soil, the Anglo-Saxons had built a large sunken hut in the area. At that time about 4ft of soil covered the floor of Room 1 and by removing half of this and a section of the north wall of the room, a semi-basement, about 20ft x 12ft was created. In this was built a wooden hut of upright boards and posts. This simple structure, largely without comfort or refinements, was typical of Anglo-Saxon houses (grubenhäuser) of the 5th-8th centuries. These were a far cry from the grandeur that was Roman Britain and indeed these early Englishmen at Dover were totally unaware of the fine floors and central heating systems which survived a few inches below their damp earth floor.

Certainly this hut was used for weaving for inside it were found nearly 200 circular, clay loomweights which served to keep vertical threads taut on a loom. These had been baked hard when the hut had eventually burned down during an extensive, totally undocumented fire.

THE PRESERVATION SCHEME

SUPPORT AND FINANCE

Following the substantial excavation of the Painted House in 1971, this important building lay buried and officially forgotten for several years. In 1975 the Kent Unit financed the re-excavation and opened the House for final public viewing. Such was the public response, however, that an appeal for funds was soon launched and the Unit devised a complete preservation-scheme for only £90,000 in contrast to the £400,000 identified officially. More than 800 Friends soon contributed £5 each and this prompted the Dover District Council and the Kent County Council each to allocate £25,000. Later the Department of Environment gave £12,500 and the Pilgrim Trust another £2,000. The project was on.

THE TRUST AND BUILDING PROGRAMME

The Painted House Trust was soon set up and a construction programme, to build a massive environmentally controlled cover-building, started in April 1976. As the contract-bids came in some £30,000 over the agreed costs the Kent Unit was obliged to become main contractor and to carry out all the heavy labour tasks and also to supervise the various sub-contractors, largely on a voluntary basis. In addition, the Unit staff designed, laid-out and prepared all the display panels and constructed the display cases. This huge task of preservation and display was completed in a non-stop 404 day operation at a final cost of only £74,000. The value of the finished scheme has been estimated at £250,000 (1976 prices) and it was opened, on schedule, on 12th May 1977.

FOUR NATIONAL AWARDS

All those who had worked so hard on the excavation and the preservation scheme were delighted that the Painted House soon won four national awards.
These were:-

1. For Outstanding Tourist Enterprise, 1977 (British Tourist Authority)

2. The Best Presentation of an Archaeological Site to the Public,1978 (Country Life)

3. The Archaeological Team showing the Greatest Initiative,1978 (Legal & General)

4. Museum of the Year Award, special prize, 1979 (Imperial Tobacco)

On completion, the scheme has been watched over by the Trust and all the staffing, management and maintenance carried out by the Kent Unit.

VISITORS AND THE QUEEN MOTHER

By 1992 nearly 400,000 visitors from 160 different countries had visited the Painted House and were delighted with the scheme. The climax came in July 1986, when Her Majesty Queen Elizabeth the Queen Mother spent more than an hour visiting the site and meeting the Trust and the Unit staff. In the years that the scheme has been open the modest admission charges have been made to cover all running costs and no public money has been used in that time. Due to the excellent management by the Kent Unit, Dover ratepayers have probably been saved over £660,000 in that time.